Design:
Tools of the Trade

by

Dr. Jack D. Kem

U.S. Army Command and General Staff College
U.S. Army Combined Arms Center
Fort Leavenworth, Kansas
May 2009

Cover Photo: U.S. Infantry and Cavalry School, Fort Leavenworth, Kansas, Class of 1907.

Foreword

The topic of *design* is vital to our Army's ability to prevail in the complex, ambiguous environment of the 21st century. Of the many lessons drawn from over seven years of wartime experience, one that stands out prominently is the critical need to improve our ability to exercise the cognitive aspects of battle command – understanding and visualizing. In this era of persistent conflict, we confront challenges that are often ill-defined and multifaceted. Where such "hybrid threats" defy convention and easy definition, traditional Cold War planning paradigms alone are insufficient. Design is not a process, but a set of "thinking tools" that complement and reinforce our operations process with a rational, logical approach to an increasingly complex and dynamic operational environment.

Design is the next step on a path to maturing our battle command model for the complexities of operations in an era of persistent conflict. It will provide future generations of leaders with the cognitive tools necessary to master our operations process at a time when our adversaries are adapting at a rate unprecedented in our history – forging an operational paradigm that is as flexible and adaptive as the leaders we are developing.

William B. Caldwell, IV
Lieutenant General, USA
Commandant, U.S. Army Command and
General Staff College

Table of Contents

Figures

Chapter Four

Chapter Five

Chapter Six

Chapter Seven

Introduction

Design is a way to help you think through handling problems – and to get others around you to help using collaboration and discourse to enable the commander's visualization of a situation.

In a collaborative environment, it is important that all – commanders as well as staff officers – bring in what they know and how they see things without being afraid to speak up. After all, even a commander doesn't know everything, even though some might not be so sure. A learning organization consisting of people with different skills and backgrounds can really help you look at problems from different perspectives – thereby assisting the commander in his mission of leading that organization.

There are nine chapters in this monograph – the first three describe design in the context of Battle Command; Chapters Four and Five discuss the key components of collaboration and reframing in Design; Chapters Six and Seven discuss some of the key terms used in Design; Chapter Eight provides an example of Design in practice; the final chapter presents some closing thoughts on Design.

If you haven't read FM 3-0, *Operations*, you're already behind – because this whole concept of design is based on several of the basic concepts from that manual – understanding, visualizing, and describing problems. If you understand those concepts from "battle command," design will make a lot more sense to you. If you do understand those concepts, Design will help you take a complex problem and let you see it for what it is so you can adjust to make things better.

Chapter One
FM 3-0 and "Understand" in Battle Command

In February 2008, the new FM 3-0, *Operations*, was published by the U.S. Army. FM 3-0 marked the first major change in Army capstone doctrine since 9/11. The manual reflected six years of wartime experience, written in response to a changing environment characterized by:

- An era of persistent conflict
- Operations among the people
- A pervasive information environment
- Unpredictable, asymmetric threats
- Conflict resolution that requires a "whole of government" approach

The "Blueprint for an Uncertain Future" that FM 3-0 provided included:

- An operational concept (full spectrum operations) that forms the core of the doctrine that focuses on initiative, risk, and opportunity while emphasizing simultaneous offense, defense, and stability operations and incorporates a broader understanding and an evolving "whole of government" approach to how we conduct stability operations

- The unparalleled power of information in contemporary operations

- The central role of the commander in an increasingly complex security environment

The central role of the commander in battle command is also strengthened in FM 3-0; the addition of the concept of "understanding" and "framing the problem" prior to "visualizing" the end state and design of the operation represents a step forward in operating in today's environment.

Not only must the commander understand the problem, he must continually reassess the environment to frame and reframe the problem. These concepts from FM 3-0, along with TRADOC PAM 525-5-500, *Commander's Appreciation and Campaign Design*, and a number of Issue Papers on the concept of design, are informing the development of FM 5-0, *The Operations Process*, which will include a chapter on design.

Not only was the role of the commander in "Battle Command" emphasized in FM 3-0, the concept of "Battle Command" was modified. The first notable change was the definition of "Battle Command."

Battle Command Definition - 2001

***Battle command* is the exercise of command in operations against a hostile, thinking enemy.** Skilled judgment gained from practice, reflection, study, experience, and intuition often guides it. The art of command lies in conscious and skillful exercise of command authority through visualization, decision making, and leadership. Using judgment acquired from experience, training, study, and creative thinking, commanders visualize the situation and make decisions. In unclear situations, informed intuition may help commanders make effective decisions by bridging gaps in information. Through the art of command, commanders apply their values, attributes, skills, and actions to lead and motivate their soldiers and units. Well-led units succeed in training and accomplish their missions. As the senior leaders of organizations, commanders apply the leadership element of combat power. Subordinate commanders and small unit leaders reinforce it.

FM 3-0 (2001), para 5-3

Figure 1-1

Battle Command Definition - 2008

Battle command **is the art and science of understanding, visualizing, describing, directing, leading, and assessing forces to impose the commander's will on a hostile, thinking, and adaptive enemy. Battle command applies leadership to translate decisions into actions—by synchronizing forces and warfighting functions in time, space, and purpose—to accomplish missions.** Battle command is guided by professional judgment gained from experience, knowledge, education, intelligence, and intuition. It is driven by commanders.

FM 3-0 (2008), para 5-9

Figure 1-2

There are several notable changes in the definitions. First, in the 2001 edition "Battle Command" was considered "principally an art that employs skills developed by professional study, constant practice, and considered judgment" (para 5-1), although Figure 5-1 in that same edition depicted a split between the "art" and "science" of war. In the 2008 edition of FM 3-0, "Battle Command" is explicitly considered both an art and science.

Second, in the 2001 edition of FM 3-0, the commander has a central role in battle command, with an emphasis on decisions the commander has to make to exercise command. Throughout the 2008 edition of FM 3-0 there is a greater emphasis on the central role of the commander, explicitly stating that Battle Command is "driven by commanders." Design reinforces this role.

Third, and probably the most evident change, is the addition of the component of "understand" in Battle Command. This component uses the tools of the operational variables (PMESII-PT) in the analysis of the context of the operational environment. Figure 1-3 shows the battle command construct from the 2001 edition of FM 3-0; Figure 1-4 shows the battle command construct from the 2008 edition of FM 3-0 with the understand component added:

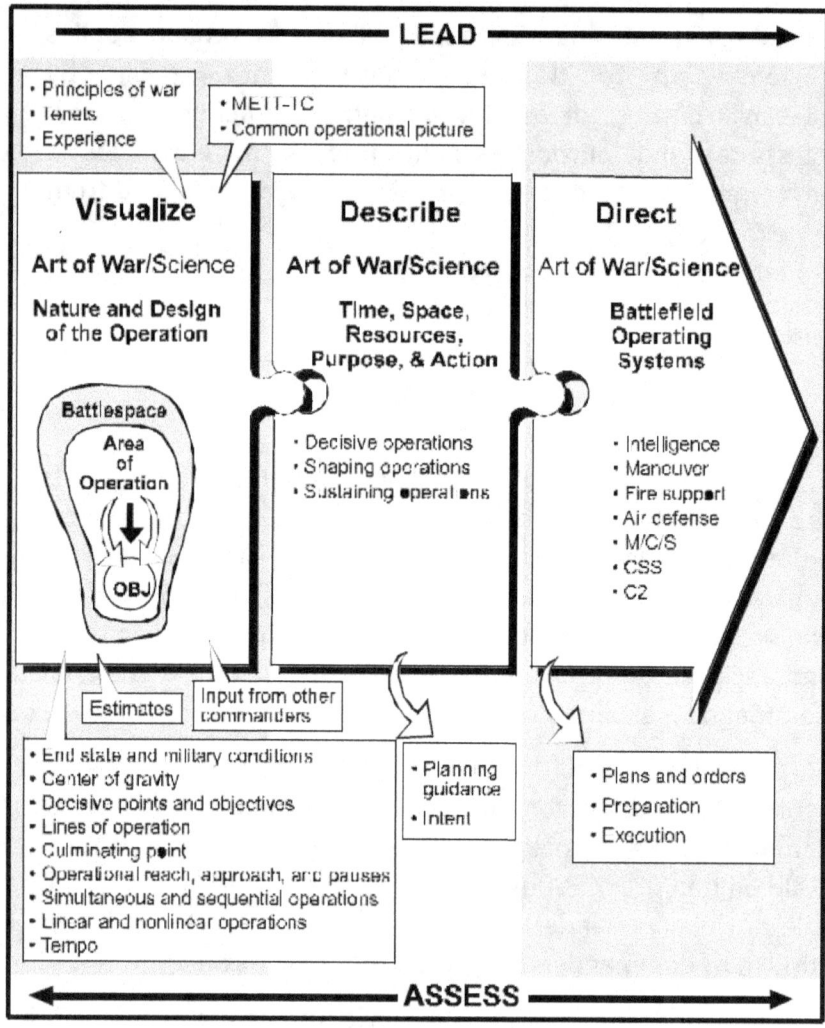

Figure 1-3

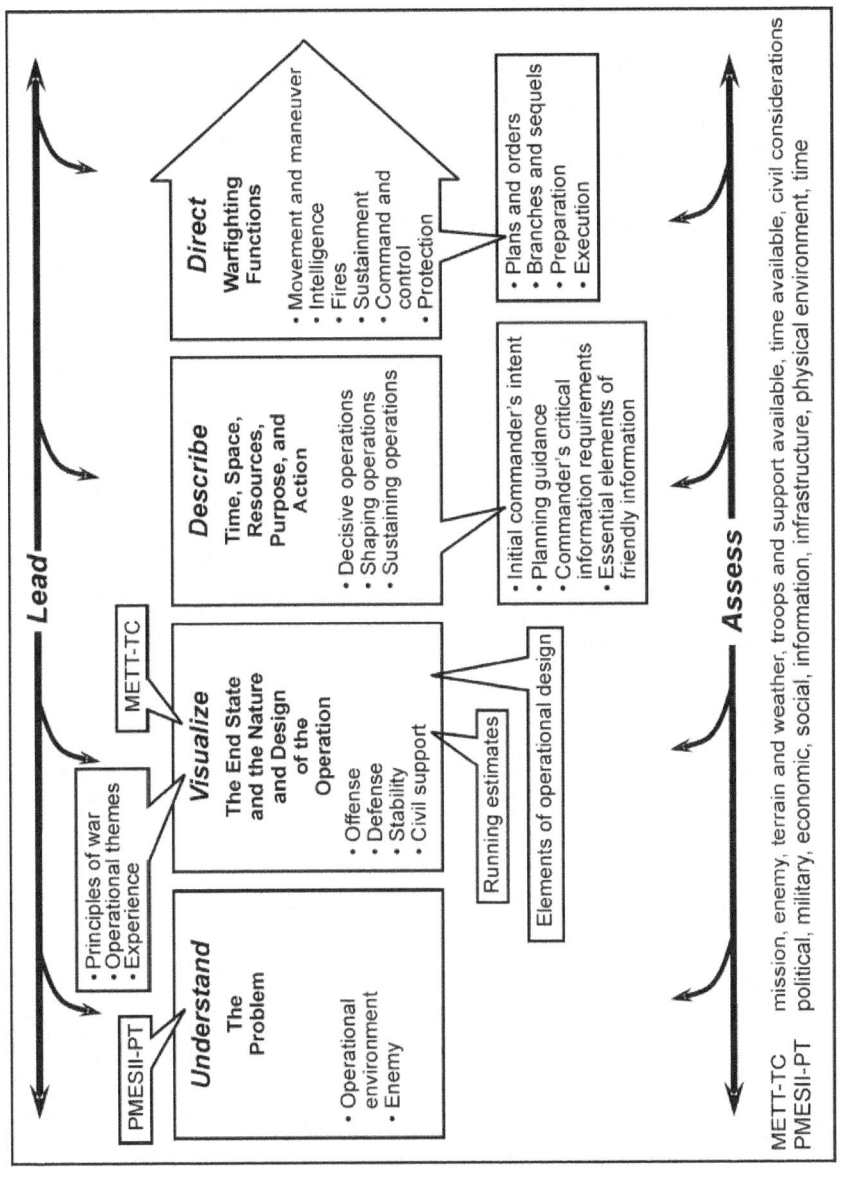

Figure 1-4

FM 3-0 (2008) also shows a depiction of how "understanding" is developed and leads to "visualization," as shown in Figure 1-5:

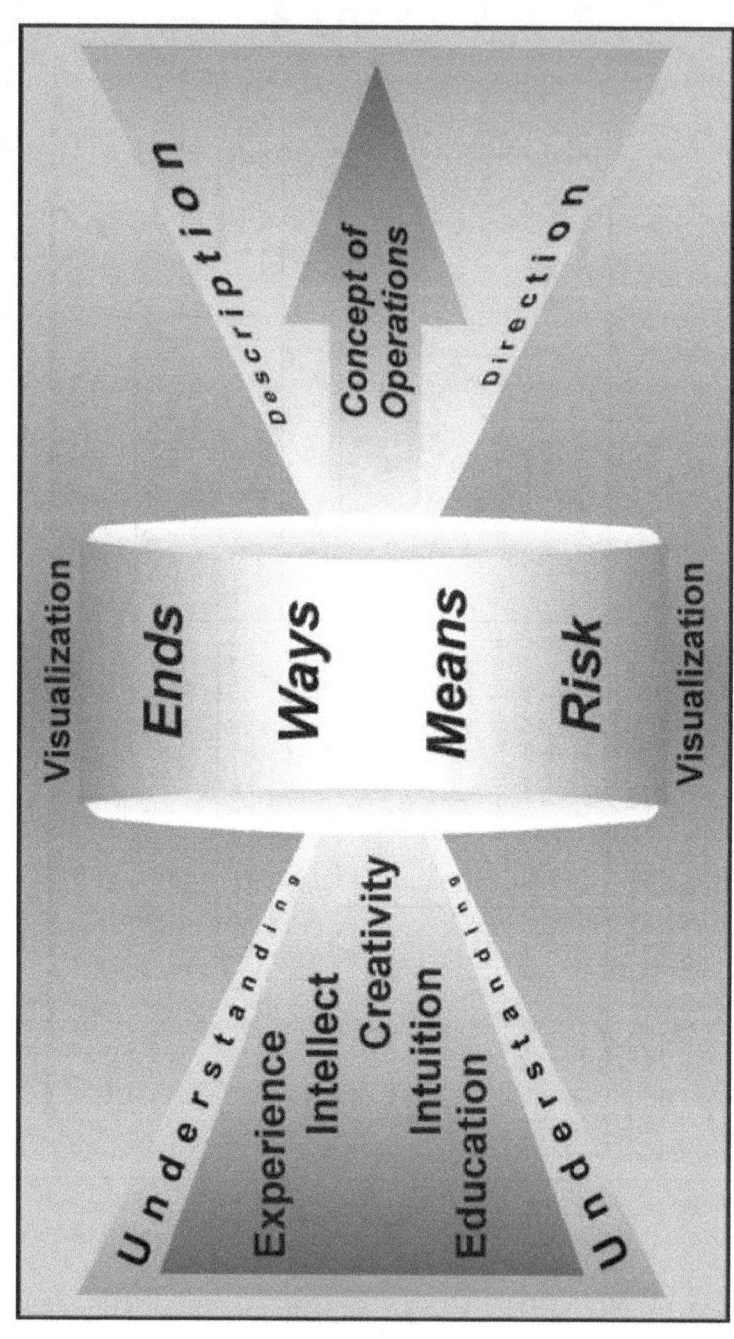

Figure 1-5

FM 3-0 (2008) provides a description of this new component of "understand" that is focused on establishing the situation's context. It is important to note that understanding is accomplished by analysis of the operational variables – and that the commander is analyzing the situation – which may not necessarily be a "new problem" at this point. The description from FM 3-0 (2008) is shown in Figure 1-6 below:

"Understanding" in Battle Command

Understanding is fundamental to battle command. It is essential to the commander's ability to establish the situation's context. Analysis of the enemy and the operational variables provides the information senior commanders use to develop understanding and frame operational problems. To develop a truer understanding of the operational environment, commanders need to circulate throughout their areas of operations as often as possible, talking to the subordinate commanders and Soldiers conducting operations, while observing for themselves. These individuals will have a more finely attuned sense of the local situation, and their intuition may cause them to detect trouble or opportunity long before the staff might. Understanding becomes the basis of the commander's visualization...

FM 3-0 (2008), para 5-16

Figure 1-6

Figures 1-3 and 1-5 depict the interaction between the components of "understanding," "visualization," and "description." FM 3-0 (2008) provides a "word picture" of this interaction, as shown in Figure 1-7:

Maintaining Understanding in Battle Command

...Maintaining <u>understanding</u> is a dynamic ability; a commander's situational understanding changes as an operation progresses. Relevant information fuels understanding and fosters initiative. Greater understanding enables commanders to make better decisions. It allows them to focus their intuition on <u>visualizing</u> the current and future conditions of the environment and <u>describe</u> them to subordinates.

FM 3-0 (2008), para 5-17

Figure 1-7

FM 3-07, *Stability Operations* (October 2008), also describes this interaction between the components of understand, visualize, and describe as shown in Figure 1-8:

Battle Command – FM 3-07

For every operation, commanders develop personal, detailed <u>understanding</u> of the situation and operational environment. They then <u>visualize</u> a desired end state and craft a broad concept for shaping the current conditions toward that end state. Finally, they <u>describe</u> their visualization through the commander's intent, planning guidance, and concept of operations, setting formal planning processes in motion.

FM 3-07 (2008), para 4-1

Figure 1-8

Chapter Six ("Operational Art") of FM 3-0 (2008) also describes the concept of <u>collaboration</u> for commanders to gain understanding of the operational context (more on this in Chapter Four):

Collaboration Informing Understanding

When applying operational art, collaboration informs situational understanding. This collaboration involves an open, continuous dialog between commanders that spans the levels of war and echelons of command. This dialog is essential to reducing the tension inherent to command and control across the levels of war. It is vital in establishing a common perspective on the problem and a shared understanding of the operational environment's conditions...

FM 3-0 (2008), para 6-21

Figure 1-9

The "Understand" component of Battle Command, therefore, is the commander's personal understanding of the context of the operational environment gained by a combination of art and science; guided by professional judgment gained from experience, knowledge, education, intelligence, and intuition; and informed by collaboration with subordinates, staffs, and commanders.

This important component of understanding the context of the operational environment in Battle Command also relates to the three activities in design: 1) understanding the current context; 2) visualizing the future context or desired end state; and 3) developing an operational approach or "theory of action" to "bridge the gap" to transform the current environment to the desired end state. The *Issue Paper: Army Design Doctrine*, 29 March 2009, emphasizes this first step of understanding the operational environment as shown in Figure 1-10:

Understanding the Environment

Design enables commanders to conceptualize the operational environment. They can visualize the environment in terms of not only enemy, adversary, friendly, and neutral systems across the spectrum of conflict, but also in the context of the political, military, economic, social, information, infrastructure, physical environment and time (PMESII-PT, FM 3-0) The commander and the design team can use the operational variables to structure the inquiry but should openly look at other ideas or dissenting opinions that may reveal other insights into the operational environment. Other subject matter area questions can expand understanding into the nuances of societal, cultural, and political variables of the local population, the physical environment, technology, local resources, and relevant history.

Issue Paper, para 2-18

Figure 1-10

As stated, the first activity in Design is conceptually the same as the first activity in Battle Command – for commanders, in their central role, to develop a personal understanding of the context of the environment to answer key questions:

What's going on?
Why has this situation developed?
What does it mean?
What's the real story?

Answering these questions helps to begin the process of understanding and framing the environment, followed by the commander's visualization of the desired end state, which will be covered in the next chapter.

Chapter Two
FM 3-0 and "Visualize" in Battle Command, Part 1

The previous chapter discussed the relationship between Design and the component of "Understand" in Battle Command. There is also an explicit link between Design and the component of "Visualize" in Battle Command.

Commander's Visualization – FM 3-0

Commander's visualization is the mental process of developing situational understanding, determining a desired end state, and envisioning the broad sequence of events by which the force will achieve that end state. It involves discussion and debate between commanders and staffs. During planning, commander's visualization provides the basis for developing plans and orders. During execution, it helps commanders determine if, when, and what to decide as they adapt to changing conditions. Commanders and staffs continuously assess the progress of operations toward the desired end state. They plan to adjust operations as required to accomplish the mission.

Subordinate, supporting, adjacent, and higher commanders communicate with one another to compare perspectives and visualize their environment. Commanders increase the breadth and depth of their visualizations by collaborating with other commanders and developing a shared situational understanding. Likewise, staff input, in the form of running estimates, focuses analysis and detects potential effects on operations. Commanders direct staffs to provide the information necessary to shape their visualization.

FM 3-0 (2008), para 5-19 – 5-20

Figure 2-1

The component of "Understanding" – the commander's personal understanding of the environment and context of the situation – forms the basis for the "Commander's Visualization." FM 3-0, *Operations* (February 2008) prescribes a new definition for the term "Commander's Visualization" as shown in Figure 2-1.

In other words, visualization builds upon understanding, as commanders continue to develop their own understanding of the situation as it develops. Commanders start to frame the problem – first, by developing a detailed understanding of the current context, answering these questions:

What's going on?
Why has this situation developed?
What does it mean?
What's the real story?

Commanders continue to frame the problem with visualization – which begins by determining the end state, or how the current conditions should be changed. In understanding, commanders used the operational variables (PMESII-PT) to assist in framing the environment; in visualization, commanders start to use mission variables (METT-TC) to assist in framing the problem.

Note that the "Commander's Visualization" is a mental process – commanders are using their own personal knowledge and intuition, as well as collaboration with subordinates, staff, and other commanders (just as they did in the understanding component of Battle Command). Commanders, in their initial stages of the "Commander's Visualization" are attempting to answer these questions:

What needs to change?
What doesn't need to change?
What are the strengths and weaknesses of the actors?
What are the opportunities and threats?
What conditions need to exist for success?

At this point, commanders continue to frame the problem by identifying an end state – a broad statement of the desired conditions that describe success. As FM 3-0 (2008) states in para 6-34, "the end state may evolve as a campaign progresses." As such, the end state is not set in concrete; at this stage commanders are identifying broad conditions that should exist in the future, informed by collaboration and discourse to determine the range of possibilities for the future.

This important component of "visualize" in Battle Command – determining the desired end state – relates directly to the activities of Design, as described in Chapter 1:

Activities of Design

Design often occurs in three activities: 1) understanding the current context; 2) visualizing the future context or desired end state; and 3) developing an operational approach or "theory of action" to "bridge the gap" to transform the current environment to the desired end state.

Figure 2-2

It is important to emphasize that the desired end state, just like current conditions, will continue to evolve and change. Current conditions change as time moves on, and therefore future desired conditions should evolve accordingly as commanders reframe and refine the desired end state. The "frame" of the problem is a "moving frame," which allows the commander to focus on future conditions. Thus, the "desired end state" is not a fixed set of conditions that cannot change – in fact, it should change to enable commanders and their subordinates to constantly assess, reframe, and reorient operations to shape and transform the future. This conceptual framework of an end state

– stated in broad terms – provides flexibility and enables initiative.

Desired End State Definition

The desired end state consists of those conditions that account for the context of the environmental frame while if achieved meet the aims of policy, orders, guidance, and directives issued to the commander. Specifically, the desired end state is the list of desired conditions that describe the prevailing context of a potential future state of affairs in the operational environment. Thus, the desired end state implies a transformation of existing conditions to desired conditions.

Issue Paper, para 2-34

Figure 2-3

After commanders have developed understanding of the situation and have determined a broad statement of the desired end state, the "Commander's Visualization" and Design move on to the next conceptual step – envisioning the broad sequence of events by which the force will achieve that end state – thereby "bridging the gap" between what exists and what should exist.

Commanders continue to frame the situation by answering the following questions:

How do we go from existing conditions to desired conditions?
What tensions exist between the two?
What else can happen?
What are the risks?

A closer look at FM 3-0 gives insight into how commanders visualize this "bridging the gap" between the current situation and the desired end state.

"Bridging the Gap"

Commander's visualization is the mental process of developing situational understanding, determining a desired end state, and envisioning the broad sequence of events by which the force will achieve that end state. It involves discussion and debate between commanders and staffs. During planning, commander's visualization provides the basis for developing plans and orders. During execution, it helps commanders determine if, when, and what to decide as they adapt to changing conditions. Commanders and staffs continuously assess the progress of operations toward the desired end state. They plan to adjust operations as required to accomplish the mission.

Subordinate, supporting, adjacent, and higher commanders communicate with one another to compare perspectives and visualize their environment. Commanders increase the breadth and depth of their visualizations by collaborating with other commanders and developing a shared situational understanding. Likewise, staff input, in the form of running estimates, focuses analysis and detects potential effects on operations. Commanders direct staffs to provide the information necessary to shape their visualization.

FM 3-0 (2008), para 5-19 – 5-20

Figure 2-4

Note that this visualization of how to "bridge the gap" includes discussion and debate between commanders and staffs, continuing the "collaboration and discourse" that characterizes Design. There is also an emphasis on adapting to current conditions, which require adjustments and adaptation in operations throughout battle command.

It is also interesting to note that this is not just a planning process; the description of the commander's visualization takes place both during planning as well as execution. Staffs provide "running estimates" to assist the commander in assessing the changes that are taking place in the environment – both the current conditions and the range of future conditions. In many ways, commander's visualization enables commanders to develop a "running commander's estimate" or what could be conceptualized as a "moving frame" which allows commanders to focus on future conditions.

As commanders visualize how to "bridge the gap" between current and desired conditions, they have a variety of tools available to enable their operational approach. These include developing key tasks or actions to be accomplished, the use of defeat or stability mechanisms, and potential lines of operation or lines of effort.

As stated in the *Issue Paper*, the main objective in Design is to "establish a broad approach to resolve a complex problem" (para A-25). Design provides the tools to understand the current context of the environment, to visualize the desired conditions, and then to develop a broad approach to bridge the gap. Commanders have framed the problem – and are now prepared to describe broadly and conceptually how to generate desirable change as part of the commander's visualization, which will be covered in the next chapter.

Chapter Three
FM 3-0 and "Describe" in Battle Command

The two previous chapters discussed the relationship between Design and the component of "Understand" in Battle Command as well as Design and the component of "Visualize" in Battle Command.

During the "understand" component of Battle Command and Design, commanders develop a clear understanding of the current context of the situation. This personal understanding of the context of the situation is gained by a combination of art and science, using professional judgment gained from experience, knowledge, education, intelligence, and intuition, and is informed by collaboration with subordinates, staffs, and commanders. Commanders answer questions such as "What's going on?" and "What's the real story?" to gain understanding of the context of the situation.

During the initial "visualize" component of Battle Command and Design, commanders visualize the desired end state – the broad statement of the desired conditions that describe success and how commanders wants to transform existing conditions. The desired end state is determined through the commander's mental evaluation of what should be transformed in the environment, bounded by the mission variables, and informed by collaboration and discourse with other commanders and staff. Commanders answer questions such as "What needs to change / what doesn't need to change?" and "What are the conditions needed for success?" to develop the desired end state.

During the "visualize" component of Battle Command and Design, commanders also visualize the broad sequence of events by which the force will achieve that end state, or how to "bridge the gap" between what exists and what should exist by determining the operational approach. The operational approach determined by the commander may include using tools such as developing key tasks or actions to be accomplished, the use of defeat or stability mechanisms, and potential lines of operation or lines of effort. Commanders continue to use collaboration and discourse as they determine the operational approach – the way the force will transform existing conditions into desired conditions. Commanders answer questions such as "How do we go from existing conditions to desired conditions?" and "What are the risks" as they develop the operational approach in framing the problem.

After commanders have framed the problem during understanding and visualization, they <u>describe</u> their commander's visualization. This is done in a variety of ways:

Describing Commander's Visualization

Commanders ... describe their visualization through the commander's intent, planning guidance, and concept of operations in a way that brings clarity to an uncertain situation.

FM 3-0 (2008), para 5-13

Figure 3-1

Note that the description in Figure 3-1 of the commander's visualization includes three different components: the commander's intent, planning guidance, and a concept of operations. FM 3-0 (2008) also provides additional guidance of how commanders should describe their visualization; in this section, the initial concept of operations is included in the planning guidance. The additional elements of information required for further planning (CCIR, which includes PIR and FFIR) and essential elements of friendly information (EEFI) are included in this description of the commander's visualization, as shown in Figure 3-2:

Initial Visualization

After commanders visualize an operation, they describe it to their staffs and subordinates to facilitate shared understanding of the mission and intent. Commanders ensure subordinates understand the visualization well enough to begin planning. Commanders describe their visualization in doctrinal terms, refining and clarifying it as circumstances require. Commanders express their initial visualization in terms of—

- Initial commander's intent.
- Planning guidance, including an initial concept of operations.
- Information required for further planning (CCIRs).
- Essential elements of friendly information (EEFIs) that must be protected.

FM 3-0 (2008), para 5-40

Figure 3-2

FM 3-0 (2008) also provides a description of the planning guidance that should accompany the initial commander's intent. The planning guidance, described as "the essence of the commander's visualization," begins to communicate how the commander visualizes resource allocation and prioritization. Although the planning guidance provides the commander's broad description of "when and where" the commander intends to use resources, the planning guidance does not give detailed guidance on "how" to use resources – which is developed later as part of the development of courses of action.

Planning Guidance – FM 3-0

Commanders provide planning guidance with their initial intent statement. Planning guidance conveys the essence of the commander's visualization. Guidance may be broad or detailed, depending on the situation. Effective planning guidance is essentially an initial concept of operations that includes priorities for each warfighting function. It reflects how the commander sees the operation unfolding. It broadly describes when, where, and how the commander intends to employ combat power to accomplish the mission within the higher commander's intent.

FM 3-0 (2008), para 5-43

Figure 3-3

The concept of planning guidance is similar in Design:

Planning Guidance – Design

The commander's planning guidance is the commander's visualization and description of the desired end state and its implications for future planning. This includes the initial commander's intent statement and reflects how the commander sees the operation unfolding. It broadly describes when, where, and how the commander intends to leverage combat power to accomplish the mission within the higher commander's intent. The planning guidance orients the focus of operations, linking desired conditions to potential combinations of actions the force may employ to achieve them.

Issue Paper, para 2-72

Figure 3-4

In Design, planning guidance is just one of the products that is prepared based on the commander's visualization. The broad guidance for the commander's visualization is given in the form of the design concept, which is the bridge between designing and planning – and during execution, between designing and execution. The design concept is described in the *Issue Paper: Army Design Doctrine*, 29 March 2009, as shown in Figure 3-5:

The Design Concept

The design concept describes the combination of conditions and actions that will guide the commander's employment of forces in concert with other instruments of power to achieve the desired end state. The design concept provides the commander's understanding of the operational environment, a description of the problem, rationale for achieving the desired end state, and implications of the design concept for future planning.

Issue Paper, para 2-57

Figure 3-5

The *Issue Paper* provides a further description of the purpose and composition of the Design Concept. There are a number of terms in the description of the Design Concept that are new terms, such as "environmental frame" and "problem frame." These terms are further defined in Chapter Six ("Key Terms"). Figure 3-6 describes the criteria for developing a "Design Concept" which is a "deliverable" of the design concept:

Design Concept Criteria

The design concept also provides criteria by which the operational approach and underlying environmental and problem frames are validated or invalidated. Design concept criteria of validation can constitute decision points for reframing. The design concept does not involve detailed planning but provides the commander's understanding of the operational environment, description of the problem, and rationale for achieving the desired end state based upon creating conditions in time and space. Along with these deliverables, the commander provides his or her initial planning guidance given the implications of the design for employing the force.

Issue Paper, para 2-58

Figure 3-6

The Design Concept is a deliberate effort to create a "deliverable" from Design that goes beyond merely "understanding." This may include planning guidance or even a formal planning directive, depending on resources available:

The Planning Directive

"...Framing the problem needs to lead to a directive, a planning directive that is then given to a planning team... So it's not a stand-alone process. It feeds into and complements what we're already doing."

Mr. Clint Ancker, Director
Combined Arms Doctrine Directorate

Figure 3-7

COL Stefan Banach, Director of SAMS, wrote an article entitled "Educating by Design: Preparing Leaders for a Complex World" in the March-April 2009 edition of *Military Review.* In this article he described some of the components of the initial planning guidance in Design as shown in Figure 3-7:

Initial Planning Directive - Design

• Initial commander's intent. The commander must provide a summary of his comprehensive visualization of the solution and what he wants to accomplish. This facilitates planning and orients the focus of operations, linking purpose to conditions that define the desired state.

• "Mission narrative." The initial expression of the command's information to describe intent to external audiences whose perceptions, attitudes, beliefs, and behaviors are relevant to the unit's mission.

• Resources. The planning directive must outline parallel efforts that must take place from other agencies and units. The command may require additional resources or need a commitment from the next higher headquarters to garner outside resources to shape the operation both within the area of responsibility and in the area of interest.

• Risk. The directive addresses risk, explaining the acceptable level of risk to seize, retain, or exploit the initiative. The design concept should also address ways to mitigate risk. FM 3-0 (para 6-102) states, "A good operational design considers risk and uncertainty equally with friction and chance."

Figure 3-8

Design moves beyond the description of the commander's visualization – design includes a design concept that "bridges" understanding and visualization, and results in planning guidance – which can be communicated as a formal planning directive.

The planning directive, if used, should include a number of items as commanders describe their visualization of the situation and provide their intent. The planning directive should include a number of components, including the commander's visualization of the situation, initial commander's intent, a broad concept of the operation, the "mission narrative," and guidance on resources and risk:

COL Stefan Banach stated in his *Military Review* article, "The planning directive is not an exclusive checklist; instead, commanders can and should adjust their planning directive's contents with each new complex situation."

The next chapter will discuss how commanders exercise collaborative leadership in order to gain this commander's visualization in an organization.

Chapter Four
Exercising Collaborative Leadership

The previous chapters on Design have addressed different components of Design as they relate to Battle Command – understanding the context of the environment, visualizing the desired future conditions or desired end state, visualizing the broad operational concept to "bridge" the current context and the desired future conditions, and using the commander's visualization and a planning directive in describing the design concept.

While using the "thinking tools" of Design, there is an emphasis on collaboration and discourse – and throughout doctrine, the terms collaboration, dialog, debate, discourse, and discussion are used frequently to characterize the interaction commanders have with staff, subordinates, and with superiors. Along this line, an interesting question was posed by one of my colleagues after our discussion of Design:

What Am I Missing?

My read of design is that THE fundamental feature that distinguishes design from engineering, construction, planning, etc. is this dialog between designer and customer. Some might argue that many healthy commanders and staffs and components already do this.... What I heard in the discussion today reiterated the top-down visualization that we see in previous doctrine... What am I missing?

Figure 4-1

He continued his questioning by referring to a paragraph in TRADOC Pam 525-5-500 (January 2008), *Commander's Appreciation and Campaign Design* (CACD):

The Flow of Understanding

Traditional planning processes implicitly assume that plans and orders from higher headquarters have framed the problem for their subordinates. CACD recognizes that orders flow from higher to lower, but understanding often flows from lower to higher, especially when operational problems are complex. In these cases, a commander is often in a better position than his superiors to understand the full scope of a complex operational problem. Thus, it is more likely that commanders at all levels will frame the problem themselves and then share their understanding with their superiors and subordinates. However, this does not mean that understanding will only flow upwards. Superiors usually have a wider perspective, which any understanding of an operational problem must take into account: where does this campaign or operation fit within the larger strategy? A significant goal of CACD is a shared understanding of complex problems. This requires battlefield circulation by higher commanders; candid discourse with superiors, subordinates, peers, and staff; and strategic thinking at all levels.

TRADOC Pam 525-5-500, para 1-1.e

Figure 4-2

This concept is still an important component of Design – collaboration "flows" both from higher to lower, as well as lower to higher and to adjacent echelons of command. Commanders collaborate in a variety of ways, including battlefield circulation, communicating with other commanders, and interacting with staffs throughout the exercise of battle command:

Battlefield Circulation

To develop a truer understanding of the operational environment, commanders need to circulate throughout their areas of operations as often as possible, talking to the subordinate commanders and Soldiers conducting operations, while observing for themselves. These individuals will have a more finely attuned sense of the local situation, and their intuition may cause them to detect trouble or opportunity long before the staff might. This deepens commanders' understanding. It allows them to anticipate potential opportunities and threats, information gaps, and capability shortfalls. Understanding becomes the basis of the commander's visualization.

FM 3-0 (2008), para 5-16

Figure 4-3

Visualization by Collaboration

Subordinate, supporting, adjacent, and higher commanders communicate with one another to compare perspectives and visualize their environment. Commanders increase the breadth and depth of their visualizations by collaborating with other commanders and developing a shared situational understanding. Likewise, staff input, in the form of running estimates, focuses analysis and detects potential effects on operations. Commanders direct staffs to provide the information necessary to shape their visualization.

FM 3-0 (2008), para 5-20

Figure 4-4

Gaining this shared understanding is essential in battle command; because greater understanding of the "reality on the ground" often flows from lower to higher echelons, this collaboration is essential. The *Issue Paper: Army Design Doctrine*, 29 March 2009, identifies that a higher echelon's understanding of a situation may be wrong by stating, "Given complex problems, guidance from higher echelons may be ambiguous, incomplete or wrong" (para A-12). The solution to this potential problem is collaboration:

Shared Understanding Through Collaboration

The commander develops a shared understanding through collaboration with superiors, peers, and subordinates. Commanders may have difficulty agreeing on the dynamics of a complex situation, but they must agree on a shared understanding of the operational environment before they can effectively frame the problem and develop solutions. This understanding ought to be shared not just laterally with other partners, but also vertically with superiors and subordinates. This will often include military and civilian leaders and other subject matter experts. Since commanders first must understand the operational environment, it is incumbent that they share this understanding with superiors early in the design methodology. This can then lead to clarification or revision of the directives or guidance that initiated design. Problem framing may reveal that doing something different is actually more appropriate than what the command was originally told to do.

Issue Paper, para A-13

Figure 4-5

So, to answer my colleague's concern, Design is not "top-driven," but incorporates the process of collaboration and discourse – up, down, and around – as a necessary component for commanders to understand and visualize.

Within a command, the commander is obviously "the central figure" in Design, and the involvement of the commander is essential. The commander, however, has to create conditions to allow for staff and subordinates to participate in healthy discourse and debate to inform the Commander's Visualization.

Discussion and Debate

Commander's visualization... involves discussion and debate between commanders and staffs...

FM 3-0 (2008), para 5-19

Figure 4-6

Creating an environment that allows for "debate" between commanders and staffs requires developing a "learning environment" with an organization:

Establishing a Collaborative Environment

...Leaders are increasingly responsible for creating environments in which individuals and organizations learn from their experiences and for establishing climates that tap the full ingenuity of subordinates. Open channels of discussion and debate are needed to encourage growth of a learning environment in which experience is rapidly shared and lessons adapted for new challenges....

FM 3-24, (2006), para 7-46

Figure 4-7

The *Issue Paper* describes collaboration as a critical component of the Design methodology. This "candid exchange of ideas without fear of retribution" is a sign of maturity in an organization – and a "hedge" against accepting a "top-down" understanding within that organization. This approach is also an important way to avoid "groupthink" in an organization:

Understanding Through Collaborative Discussion

The commander creates understanding through collaborative discussion. Collaboration is an essential technique for learning. Collaboration is the candid exchange of ideas without fear of retribution that results in a synthesis and a shared understanding of operational problems...

The commander creates conditions that allow participants to think critically and creatively and share their ideas and recommendations through collaboration. Groupthink is the antithesis of healthy collaboration and design. A zero defects command climate will stifle learning since successful collaboration requires candor and a free yet mutually respectful competition of opposing ideas. Participants must feel free to take minority viewpoints based on their expertise, experience, and insight; this includes sharing ideas that contradict the opinions held by those of higher rank....

Issue Paper, para A-4 – A-5

Figure 4-8

As the *Issue Paper* describes, Design "provides an opportunity to convert intellectual power into combat power" (para 1-26). In order to accomplish this, commanders must resist the temptation to be directive, but instead must practice collaborative leadership:

The Practice of Collaborative Leadership

Design requires the practice of a collaborative leadership. This type of leadership engages in continuing dialog, leading to increased understanding and a sense of participation in the commander's decisionmaking. The collaborative leadership involves subordinate commanders, representatives of various staff disciplines, military and civilian, joint and multinational forces, and the higher commander.

Issue Paper, para 1-29

Figure 4-9

The next chapter will discuss a key element of Design – the issue of framing and reframing.

Chapter Five
Framing and Reframing

The previous chapter on Design discussed the issue of exercising collaborative leadership in Design; this is a key element in developing the initial design concept – understanding the context of the environment, visualizing the desired future conditions / desired end state, visualizing the broad operational concept to "bridge" the current context and the desired future conditions, and using the commander's visualization and a planning directive in describing the design concept.

As mentioned in previous chapters, current conditions change as time moves on, and therefore future desired conditions should evolve accordingly as commanders reframe and refine the desired end state, resulting in a refined operational concept. This creates a "frame" of the problem that is a "moving frame," or in essence a "running commander's estimate." This leads to several questions: When should a commander reframe? What should "trigger" a reframing of the problem?

Part of the answer rests in assessment. FM 3-0, Operations (2008) provides some discussion on the component of assessment in Battle Command:

Assessment in Battle Command

...To ensure progress toward the end state, higher level commanders continuously assess the overall campaign and their subordinates' operations. They adjust the type of operation as each campaign phase unfolds.

FM 3-0 (2008), para 2-14

Figure 5-1

The description in Figure 5-1 from FM 3-0 indicates assessment as a tool to inform a response and reaction to current conditions, rather than using assessment as a tool to inform reframing of the problem. Reframing, if it follows the same process as framing, would not only inform the understanding of the current context, but would also force a "reframed" visualization of the end state and the operational approach.

Some more examples from FM 3-0 (2008):

Progress Toward the Desired End State

...Commanders and staffs continuously assess the progress of operations toward the desired end state. They plan to adjust operations as required to accomplish the mission.

FM 3-0 (2008), para 5-19

Figure 5-2

The process of reframing does not focus on "progress toward the end state," but forces a new visualization of the desired conditions for the end state. The adjustment isn't just for operations as they continue; the adjustment may include a new determination of the end state and the operational approach.

Situational Understanding

...Commanders make decisions and direct actions based on their situational understanding, which they maintain by continuous assessment....

FM 3-0 (2008), para 5-52

Figure 5-3

The process of reframing does not inform commanders to make decisions solely upon their situational understanding; reframing informs commanders to make decisions based on their visualization of both situational understanding of the context and visualization of the future.

Remaining Focused on the Situation

Assessment is the continuous monitoring and evaluation of the current situation, particularly the enemy, and progress of an operation. Commanders, assisted by their staffs and subordinate commanders, continuously assess the current situation and the progress of the operation and compare it with the concept of operations, mission, and commander's intent. Based on their assessment commanders direct adjustments, ensuring that the operation remains focused on the mission and commander's intent.

FM 3-0 (2008), para 5-84

Figure 5-4

Finally, the process of reframing does not cause commanders to compare actions with the existing concept of operations and commanders intent, but instead forces a "relook" of those components.

FM 3-0 (2008) specifically mentions <u>reframing</u> in only two places – and both times the concept is mentioned in conjunction with the concept of framing. This brief treatment does not describe when a commander should reframe a problem, but instead just "lumps" reframing in with framing:

Reframing – FM 3-0

Framing (and reframing) the problem encompasses receiving and clarifying the strategic end state and conditions. It also includes determining the appropriate operational theme, operational approach, and defeat or stability mechanisms. Framing requires understanding and viewing the operational environment from a systemic perspective and identifying and analyzing centers of gravity. Collaboration informs problem framing.

FM 3-0 (2008), para 6-30

Figure 5-5

The *Issue Paper: Army Design Doctrine*, 29 March 2009, discusses the issue of reframing. Design methodology surfaces assumptions about the problem, assessing whether the approach is "solving the right problem" (*Issue Paper*, para 1-19). One of the key components in Design that assists in determining if reframing is necessary is to determine "reframing criteria" –

Solving the Right Problem

...A design concept that provides reframing criteria enables commanders to better respond to unforeseen challenges and maintain relevance... The design concept ... assesses the possible effects of actions, establishing criteria to help determine whether changes are needed, and how changes impact the decision to reframe all or part of the overall design.

Issue Paper, para 2-76

Figure 5-6

Reframing in a Learning Organization

...the commander must lead the learning in an organization and develop ways to gain information to determine if reframing of the problem or design concept is necessary... As the operational environment, complex problems, and desired conditions change, leaders monitor the criteria they establish for reframing...

Issue Paper, para 2-80

Figure 5-7

The *Issue Paper* also provides some insight into some of the potential factors that can inform the criteria for reframing:

Restarting Design

Reframing is restarting the design after discarding the hypotheses or theories which defined either or both the environmental frame or the problem frame. The commander makes the decision to reframe when changes in the operational environment render the operational approach no longer feasible, acceptable, or suitable in the context of higher policy, orders, guidance, or directives. The commander may base this decision on the design concept or operational approach failing to meet the criteria listed above. Another example of reframing is when commanders can no longer explain actor behavior in the operational environment.

Issue Paper, para 2-81

Figure 5-8

In addition, the *Issue Paper* also brings out an important concept – that reframing is not only important when things are not going well; it is equally important in the "wake of success."

Reframing in the Wake of Success

Reframing may be equally important in the wake of success. By its very nature, success transforms the environment and affects its tendencies, potentials, and tensions. Organizations are strongly motivated to reflect and reframe following failure, but they tend to neglect reflection and reframing following successful actions...

Issue Paper, para 2-83

Figure 5-9

The questions from above that are still to be answered are: "When should a commander reframe?" "What should "trigger" a reframing of the problem?" Commanders should reframe constantly; as a mental process, commanders should be asking questions throughout planning and operations such as:

What's the real story right now? Has this changed?
What are the strengths and weaknesses of the actors? Has this changed?
What are the opportunities and threats? Has this changed?
What are the conditions needed for success? Has this changed?
How do we go from existing conditions to desired conditions? Has this changed?
What else can happen? Has this changed?
What are the risks? Has this changed?

Commanders may want to develop "reframing criteria" – measures that indicate when there has been significant change that should force a reframing. Establishing these measures will require practice and discipline, because the normal tendency will be to continue to "fight the plan" rather than conditions.

Another technique commanders may want to consider is the "red-team" concept – that is, dedicating staff officers to continually assess conditions, both current and future, to determine if the command is framing the right problem. Integrating this concept of Design into an organization will be difficult because it requires a change in mindset to stay adaptive and flexible – but this change is essential for success.

TRADOC Pam 525-5-500 (January 2008), *Commander's Appreciation and Campaign Design* (CACD), puts the issue of reframing in context by stating that the initial framing of a problem is just the start point:

Reframing in Context

"...the initial framing of the problem establishes only a starting hypothesis and a baseline for learning about the problem as the force operates. It sets the parameters for reframing—readjusting the commander's appreciation of the problem—as the commander's understanding expands and the situation changes over time...."

TRADOC Pam 525-5-500, para 1-6.b

Figure 5-10

The *Issue Paper: Army Design Doctrine* (29 March 2009) states that "Leaders always need to direct some attention toward problem framing; they need to ask whether they really are solving the right problem." The difficulty is determining if commanders are "working the wrong problem" and should conduct reframing. The TRADOC Pamphlet on *Commander's Appreciation and*

Campaign Design (CACD) provides some insight of the difficulty of determining when a commander should reframe a problem:

Change and Adaptation

Change and adaptation will and must occur for the campaign design to remain relevant to the assigned strategic aims. A significant issue for the commander during a campaign is to determine when his understanding of the operational problem might change—either because he has learned more or because the problem itself has fundamentally changed.

TRADOC Pam 525-5-500, para 3-1.d.(3)(a)

Figure 5-11

Determining when to reframe is more "art" than "science." Because the current context is always changing and evolving, the problem frame is evolving... knowing when an operation (or planning) is "on track" or needs to be "scrapped" is tough:

Meaningful Adaptation

The commander's framing and understanding of the operational environment will evolve as his forces conduct operations over the duration of the campaign. The key point of art for the commander is to determine when his understanding has developed enough to allow him to make a meaningful adaptation of the campaign design or to scrap the design in favor of a more effective approach.

TRADOC Pam 525-5-500, para 3-1.d.(3)(b)

Figure 5-12

One of the potential solutions described earlier in this chapter was to develop "reframing criteria." The concept of "reframing criteria" is not the same as CCIR, because CCIR support a commander's ability to act and are tied to decisions. In contrast, reframing criteria should support the commander's ability to understand, learn, and adapt – and reframe as necessary. As TRADOC Pam 525-5-500 para 3-1.d.(3)(c) states, reframing criteria should "cue the commander to rethink his understanding of the operational environment, and hence rethink how to solve the problem(s)."

There are three different potential approaches to developing the "triggers" for reframing criteria:

* Catastrophic Events: A major event causes a "catastrophic change" in the environment that necessitates reframing the problem. Examples would include the 9/11 attack, the attack in Samarra, and the Anbar Awakening... these events clearly changed the situation and required comprehensive reframing of the problem.

* Periodic Review: Commanders need to schedule a time where reframing takes place. At the strategic level, major OPLANS are normally reviewed every two years; at the operational and tactical level, Battle Update Assessments (BUAs) provide an opportunity to review "where you are and where you are going" on a regular basis. These periodic reviews can form an opportunity to reframe the problem through focused, deliberate action.

* Constant Reflection: As the *Issue Paper* states in para 1-30, "Design requires the commander to lead adaptive work...the commander must lead the learning in an organization... This requires continual assessment, evaluation, and reflection that challenge how commanders understand the existing problem and the relevance of actions addressing that problem." Commanders

and staff should continually assess and reflect on the problem, constantly asking the nagging question, "Are we solving the right problem?" This reflection should become apparent when you realize that "the enemy we're fighting is not the enemy we'd wargamed against."

The next chapter, Chapter Six, will discuss some of the key terms that are used in Design.

Chapter Six
Key Terms

The concept of Design has a number of terms that are used to describe different components. Some of the key terms used in Design are: Environmental Frame; Problem Frame; Problem Statement; Operational Approach (the theory of action); and Design Concept.

There are a number of sources to draw upon to gain insight into how these terms are defined and used, including the *Issue Paper: Army Design Doctrine* (29 March 2009); "Educating by Design: Preparing Leaders for a Complex World" by COL Stefan J. Banach in the March-April 2009 *Military Review*; and "The Art of Design: A Design Methodology" by COL Stefan J. Banach and Dr. Alex Ryan in the March-April 2009 *Military Review*.

Environmental Frame: The environmental frame is the "big picture" that describes, in both graphic and narrative form, the historical context, current conditions, and potential future conditions of the environment.   The environmental frame emphasizes the flows and relationships between the actors in the environment, using tools such as PMESII-PT.   During Battle Command, the environmental frame is determined during the "understand" component and during the "visualize" component when identifying the band of conditions that comprise the desired end state. The environmental frame identifies the "big picture" context of the operational environment – how the context developed (historical perspective), how the context currently exists (current conditions), and how the context could trend in the future (future conditions or desired end state).   The environmental frame should include the commander's areas of operations, influence, and interest.

Problem Frame: The problem frame is a refinement of the environmental frame that describes, in both graphic and narrative form, the specific areas of action that will move existing conditions toward the desired end state, or, in other words, the areas where "bridging the gap" actions to transform the current environment to the desired end state will take place. The problem frame captures the broad aspects of the environment that are relevant to the problem, setting the boundaries for action (using the mission variables of METT-TC). The problem frame goes beyond identifying flows and relationships in the environment; the problem frame identifies areas of tension and competition (as well as opportunities and challenges) that must be addressed in order to transform current conditions to achieve the desired end state.

Problem Statement: The problem statement must clearly define the problem that must be managed or solved. The problem statement considers the impact of tension and competition in the environment by identifying how to take the current conditions to the friendly desired end state – before an adversary or competitor takes current conditions to their desired end state. The problem statement should take into account the time and space relationships that are inherent in the problem frame, as well as tension and competition within the operational context; the problem statement must address the "essence of success." The problem statement draws attention to achieving a competitive advantage. In highlighting competitive advantage, the problem statement helps planners understand the temporal nature of the relationship between opposing sides. Problems that involve military forces tend to be a race for competitive advantage: for example, against a political power, against a military force, against an insurgency, or against a force of nature.

Operational Approach (Theory of Action): The operational approach, or theory of action, is a hypothesis – the broad approach to resolving the problem. The operational approach is not a course of action, but instead a broad approach that provides insight into how to solve the problem. The operational approach should address the problem statement in two ways: first, to reinforce positive actions that support the desired end state; and second, to suggest actions to counter negative actions to overcome anticipated resistance to the desired end state. The operational approach (theory of action) should provide broad conceptual coherence to unify the environmental frame, the problem frame, and the design concept.

Design Concept: The design concept, communicated in graphic and narrative form, consists of the commander's intent and planning guidance, or a planning directive. The design concept is communicated with a number of products, including:

• Initial commander's intent. A summary of the commander's comprehensive visualization of the conditions comprising the desired end state to provide focus for operations. The initial commander's intent should include the initial concept of operations, reflecting how the commander sees the operation unfolding. Commanders may use lines of effort, key tasks, and defeat or stability mechanisms to communicate their initial commander's intent.

• "Mission narrative." The initial expression of the command's information to describe intent to external audiences whose perceptions, attitudes, beliefs, and behaviors are relevant to the unit's mission. The "mission narrative" should articulate conditions, opportunities, key actions and potential payoffs (The "mission narrative" is discussed in the next chapter).

• Resources. The planning directive must outline parallel efforts that must take place from other agencies and units, as well as from other instrument of national power. Additional resources that are required from outside the command should be identified.

• Risk. The design concept should address risk and uncertainty, providing guidance on the acceptable level of risk to seize, retain, or exploit the initiative.

Figure 6-1 is from the article by COL Stefan J. Banach and Dr Alex entitled "The Art of Design: A Design Methodology" in the March-April 2009 edition of *Military Review*. The Figure is a graphic portrayal of the five concepts within this chapter:

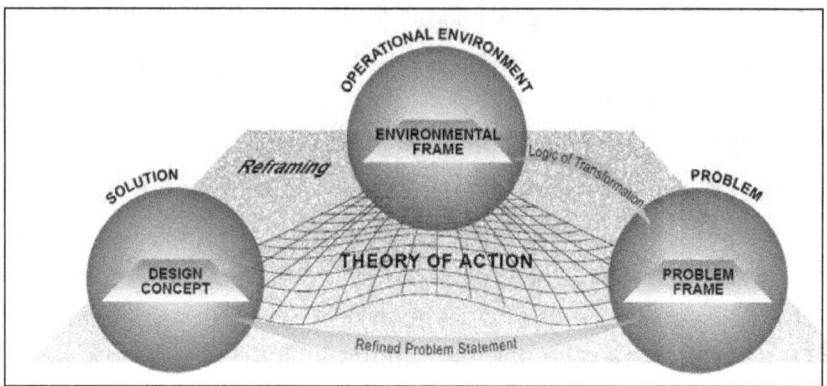

Figure 6-1

- The **Environmental Frame** as the description of the "big picture" of the operational environment;

- The **Problem Frame** as the description of the problem, with the "logic of transformation" that will move existing conditions toward the desired end state;

- The **Operational Approach** or **Theory of Action** as the insight into how to resolve the problem;

- The **Problem Statement** that defines the problem that must be managed or solved; and

- The **Design Concept** that presents the solution to the problem communicated in the planning guidance or planning directive.

The next chapter, Chapter Seven, will discuss the concept of the "Mission Narrative."

Chapter Seven
The "Mission Narrative"

One component that is relatively new in doctrine is the concept of the "mission narrative." FM 3-13, *Information* (Initial Draft), 27 February 2009, provides the following draft definition:

"Mission Narrative" Definition – FM 3-13 (ID)

A mission narrative is a single narrative statement made by the commander, published within base plans, articulating the conditions, opportunity, key actions and payoffs associated with a particular mission. The mission narrative is constructed for the purposes of providing common 'azimuth' for subordinate Army forces and Soldiers to communicate effectively and accurately to critical publics and actors. Mission Narratives ideally arise from a collaborative effort that truthfully and accurately reflects what the mission itself is likely to communicate or signal to those publics observing it. Since any mission's success is largely dependent on the 'story' it communicates, prospective mission narratives may be used as criteria on which to evaluate the feasibility, suitability, acceptability, and distinguishability of specific courses of action. At the operational level, the mission narrative is expressed as the campaign narrative.

FM 3-13 (ID), para 6-31

Figure 7-1

The "mission narrative" is distinct from the commander's intent; the commander's intent focuses on internal actions of the force and addresses the components of "what" and "so what" with key tasks, end state, and purpose. The commander's intent guides subordinates in knowing what they have to do (key tasks), why they are doing it (purpose), what success looks like (end state), and how actions fit into the larger plan (linkage).

The "mission narrative," on the other hand, focuses on the external audiences, emphasizing the "payoff" from their perspective. The "mission narrative" addresses the components of "which means" and "therefore," focusing on perceptions, attitudes, beliefs, and behaviors of external audiences. Subordinates' actions are guided by the "mission narrative" (just as they are guided by the commander's intent), but the "mission narrative" is intended to look how key actions and their payoffs are perceived "in the shoes" of external audiences observing those actions.

"Mission Narrative" – Proposed Definition

The Mission Narrative is a single narrative statement made by the commander that articulates conditions, opportunities, key actions and potential payoffs associated with a particular mission. At the campaign level, the mission narrative is described as the campaign narrative. The mission narrative is developed to provide a common 'azimuth' to communicate effectively and accurately to external audiences, whose perceptions, attitudes, beliefs, and behaviors are relevant to the unit's mission. Mission Narratives should be developed from a collaborative effort that truthfully and accurately reflects what the mission itself is likely to communicate to those external audiences. Since any mission's success is largely dependent on the 'story' it communicates, mission narratives should be analyzed as part of the evaluation process when comparing specific courses of action."

Figure 7-2

Developing a "mission narrative" should be an essential component of design, drawing heavily on collaboration and discourse and knowledge of current perceptions in the operational environment. Using the construct of conditions, opportunities, key actions and potential payoffs, the figure below shows the general construction of a "mission narrative":

Figure 7-3

Figure 7-3 provides a schematic to guide how to develop a "mission narrative." The "mission narrative" should consist of a series of statements of 150 words or less that can be communicated in no more than a minute. The start point for the "mission narrative" should be a statement of the current conditions (informed by the commander's understanding of the environment and easily understood by listeners). Based on these conditions, there should be a statement of the opportunities that are presented by the environment that permits change and transformation to better conditions. In response to these opportunities, there will be a number of key actions that will be observed by external audiences. These actions will result in different payoffs – for some audiences, the payoffs will be positive; for others (primarily adversaries), the payoff will be negative. The payoffs will result in a new set of conditions – the transformed context.

They key component in the "mission narrative" – the important part of the "story" – is in communicating the payoff for external audiences.

President Obama's Inaugural Address provides an example of a strategic level "mission narrative" – excerpts from his address indicate the components of the "mission narrative" and an emphasis on payoffs:

> ...Our nation is at war against a far-reaching network of violence and hatred... (<u>Conditions</u>)

> ...earlier generations faced down fascism and communism not just with missiles and tanks, but with the sturdy alliances and enduring convictions. ...we can meet those new threats that demand even greater effort, even greater cooperation and understanding between nations... (<u>Opportunities</u>)

> We will begin to responsibly leave Iraq to its people and forge a hard-earned peace in Afghanistan. With old friends and former foes, we'll work tirelessly to lessen the nuclear threat, and roll back the specter of a warming planet. (<u>Key Actions</u>)

> ...For those who seek to advance their aims by inducing terror and slaughtering innocents...you cannot outlast us, and we will defeat you; To those leaders around the globe who seek to sow conflict, or blame their society's ills on

the West, know that your people will judge you on what you can build, not what you destroy; To those who cling to power through corruption and deceit and the silencing of dissent, know that you are on the wrong side of history, but that we will extend a hand if you are willing to unclench your fist...; To the people of poor nations, we pledge to work alongside you to make your farms flourish and let clean waters flow; to nourish starved bodies and feed hungry minds... (Payoffs)

The Center for a New American Security (CNAS) published a monograph by MG (Ret) Robert H. Scales entitled "The Past and Present as Prologue: Future Warfare through the Lens of Contemporary Conflicts" in April 2009. On page 21 of the monograph MG (Ret) Scales states:

Today's Challenge

"...today's challenge is to develop another generation of soldiers equally skilled in the narrative arts. Skill at feeding the narrative is no longer a contributor to achieving strategic success in irregular war. It is in fact the principle determinant, and the psychological center of gravity, for shaping the perceptions and influencing the will of the population. The "area of operations" concept has given way to a narrative stream defined by the global media. While the narrative stream is neutral, who occupies and exploits it is not. In the end, "ground truth" or actual battlefield conditions will prevail. In this new American era of warfare, however, the art of feeding the operational narrative requires skill in maneuvering across the expanse of human perception rather than an expanse of territory."

MG (Ret) Robert H. Scales

Figure 7-4

Chapter Eight
Design in Action: General Ridgway in Korea

Chapter Six of FM 22-100, *Army Leadership: Be, Know, Do* (August 1999), contained a historical case study of General Matthew Ridgway in Korea in paragraphs 6-142 through 6-161 that provides insight into Design. Although FM 22-100 has been superseded by FM 6-22, the case study illustrates how the concept of Design is timeless.

The case study is included in its entirety; underlined passages are for emphasis to indicate components of design:

6-142. Few leaders have better exemplified effective organizational leadership in combat than GEN Matthew B. Ridgway. GEN Ridgway successfully led the 82d Airborne Division and XVIII Airborne Corps in the ETO during World War II and Eighth (US) Army during the Korean War. His actions during four months in command of Eighth Army prior to his appointment as UN Supreme Commander bring to life the skills and actions described throughout this chapter.

6-143. At the outbreak of the Korean War in June 1950, GEN Ridgway was assigned as the Army Deputy Chief of Staff, Operations. In an agreement between the Army Chief of Staff, GEN J. Lawton Collins, and the UN Supreme Commander, GA Douglas MacArthur, GEN Ridgway was identified early as the replacement for the Eighth Army commander, GEN Walton H. Walker, in the event GEN Walker was killed in combat.

6-144. That year, on 23 December, GEN Walker died in a jeep accident. Following approval by Secretary of Defense George C. Marshall and President Truman, GEN Ridgway was ordered to take command of Eighth Army. At that time, Eighth Army was defending near the 38th parallel, having completed a 300-mile retreat after the Chinese intervention and stunning victory on the Chongchin River.

6-145. The UN defeat had left its forces in serious disarray. One of Eighth Army's four American divisions, the 2d, needed extensive replacements and reorganization. Two other divisions, the 25th and 1st Cavalry, were seriously battered. Of the Republic of Korea divisions, only the 1st was in good fighting shape. A British brigade was combat ready, but it too had suffered substantial losses in helping cover the retreat.

6-146. Within 24 hours of GEN Walker's death, GEN Ridgway was bound for Korea. During the long flight from Washington, DC, to GA MacArthur's headquarters in Japan, GEN Ridgway had an opportunity to reflect on what lay ahead. He felt this problem was like so many others he had experienced: "Here's the situation—what's your solution?" He began to formulate his plan of action. He determined each step based on his assessment of the enemy's strengths and capabilities as well as his own command's strengths and capabilities.

> Note: Reflection, intuition of the commander, informed by assessment of strengths and weaknesses

6-147. The necessary steps seemed clear: gain an appreciation for the immediate situation from GA MacArthur's staff, establish his presence as Eighth Army commander by sending a statement of his confidence in them, and then meet with his own staff to establish his priorities. His first message to his new command was straight to the point: "You will have my utmost. I shall expect yours."

> Note: Collaboration with higher staff; meeting with his own staff to gain an appreciation of the situation.

6-148. During the flight from Japan to his forward command post, GEN Ridgway carefully looked at the terrain upon which he was to fight. The battered Eighth Army had to cover a rugged, 100-mile-long front that restricted both maneuver and resupply.

Poor morale presented a further problem. Many military observers felt that Eighth Army lacked spirit and possessed little stomach for continuing the bruising battle with the Chinese.

Note: Initial PMESII-PT analysis

6-149. For three days GEN Ridgway traveled the army area by jeep, talking with commanders who had faced the enemy beyond the Han River. GEN Ridgway wrote later, *I held to the old-fashioned idea that it helped the spirits of the men to see the Old Man up there, in the snow and the sleet and the mud, sharing the same cold, miserable existence they had to endure.*

Note: Battlefield circulation

6-150. GEN Ridgway believed a commander should publicly show a personal interest in the well-being of his soldiers. He needed to do something to attract notice and display his concern for the front-line fighters. Finding that one of his units was still short of some winter equipment, GEN Ridgway dramatically ordered that the equipment be delivered within 24 hours. In response, the logistical command made a massive effort to comply, flying equipment from Pusan to the front lines. Everyone noticed. He also ordered—and made sure the order was known—that the troops be served hot meals, with any failures to comply reported directly to him.

Note: Continued Battlefield circulation

6-151. GEN Ridgway was candid, criticizing the spirit of both the commanders and soldiers of Eighth Army. He talked with riflemen and generals, from front-line foxholes to corps command posts. He was appalled at American infantrymen who didn't patrol, who had no knowledge of the terrain in which they fought, and who failed to know the whereabouts of their enemy.

Moreover, this army was roadbound and failed to occupy commanding terrain overlooking its positions and supply lines. GEN Ridgway also sensed that Eighth Army—particularly the commanders and their staffs—kept looking over their shoulders for the best route to the rear and planned only for retreat. In short, he found his army immobilized and demoralized.

> Note: Candor, continued assessment of the situation

6-152. An important part of GEN Ridgway's effort to instill fighting spirit in Eighth Army was to order units to close up their flanks and tie in with other units. He said he wanted no units cut off and abandoned, as had happened to the 3d Battalion, 8th Cavalry at Unsan, Task Force Faith at Chosin Reservoir, and the 2d Division at Kuni-ri. GEN Ridgway felt that it was essential for soldiers to know they would not be left to fend for themselves if cut off. He believed that soldiers would be persuaded to stand and fight only if they realized help would come. Without that confidence in the command and their fellow soldiers, they would pull out, fearing to be left behind.

> Note: Visualization of the problem in 8th Army and identification of new conditions to be established

6-153. As he visited their headquarters, GEN Ridgway spoke to commanders and their staffs. These talks contained many of his ideas about proper combat leadership. He told his commanders to get out of their command posts and up to the front. When commanders reported on terrain, GEN Ridgway demanded that they base their information on personal knowledge and that it be correct.

> Note: Collaboration; description of intent; continued situational understanding

6-154. Furthermore, he urged commanders to conduct intensive training in night fighting and make full use of their firepower. He also required commanders to personally check that their men had adequate winter clothing, warming tents, and writing materials. In addition, he encouraged commanders to locate wounded who had been evacuated and make every effort to return them to their old units. Finally, the army commander ordered his officers to stop wasting resources, calling for punishment of those who lost government equipment.

6-155. During its first battle under GEN Ridgway's command in early January 1951, Eighth Army fell back another 70 miles and lost Seoul, South Korea's capital. Major commanders didn't carry out orders to fall back in an orderly fashion, use field artillery to inflict the heaviest possible enemy casualties, and counterattack in force during daylight hours. Eighth Army's morale and sense of purpose reached their lowest point ever.

6-156. Eighth Army had only two choices: substantially improve its fighting spirit or get out of Korea. GEN Ridgway began to restore his men's fighting spirit by ordering aggressive patrolling into areas just lost. When patrols found the enemy few in number and not aggressive, the army commander increased the number and size of patrols. His army discovered it could drive back the Chinese without suffering overwhelming casualties. Buoyed by these successes, GEN Ridgway ordered a general advance along Korea's west coast, where the terrain was more open and his forces could take advantage of its tanks, artillery, and aircraft.

> Note: Identification of range of "end states"

6-157. During this advance, GEN Ridgway also attempted to tell the men of Eighth Army why they were fighting in Korea. He sought to build a fighting spirit in his men based on unit and soldier pride. In addition, he called on them to defend Western

Civilization from Communist degradation, saying: *In the final analysis, the issue now joined right here in Korea is whether Communism or individual freedom shall prevail; whether the flight of the fear-driven people we have witnessed here shall be checked, or shall at some future time, however distant, engulf our own loved ones in all its misery and despair.*

> Note: The "Mission Narrative"

6-158. In mid-February of 1951, the Chinese and North Koreans launched yet another offensive in the central area of Korea, where US tanks could not maneuver as readily and artillery could be trapped on narrow roads in mountainous terrain. In heavy fights at Chipyon-ni and Wonju, Eighth Army, for the first time, re-repulsed the Communist attacks. Eighth Army's offensive spirit soared as GEN Ridgway quickly followed up with a renewed attack that took Seoul and regained roughly the same positions Eighth Army had held when he first took command. In late March, Eighth Army pushed the Communist forces north of the 38th parallel.

> Note: Reframing – new end state conditions

6-159. GEN Ridgway's actions superbly exemplify those expected of organizational leaders. His knowledge of American soldiers, units, and the Korean situation led him to certain expectations. Those expectations gave him a baseline from which to assess his command once he arrived. He continually visited units throughout the army area, talked with soldiers and their commanders, assessed command climate, and took action to mold attitudes with clear intent, supreme confidence, and unyielding tactical discipline.

6-160. He sought to develop subordinate commanders and their staffs by sharing his thoughts and expectations of combat leadership. He felt the pulse of the men on the front, shared their hardships, and demanded they be taken care of. He pushed the logistical systems to provide creature comforts as well as the supplies of war. He <u>eliminated the skepticism of purpose, gave soldiers cause to fight, and helped them gain confidence by winning small victories.</u> Most of all, he led by example.

> <u>Note</u>: Constant collaboration; providing new purpose and end state; developing an operational approach / theory of action for success

6-161. In April GEN Ridgway turned Eighth Army over to GEN James A. Van Fleet. In under four months, a dynamic, aggressive commander had revitalized and transformed a traumatized and desperate army into a proud, determined fighting force. GA Omar N. Bradley, Chairman of the Joint Chiefs of Staff, summed up GEN Ridgway's contributions: *It is not often that a single battlefield commander can make a decisive difference. But in Korea Ridgway would prove to be that exception. His brilliant, driving, uncompromising leadership would turn the tide of battle like no other general's in our military history.*

Chapter Nine
Closing Thoughts

There are a number of reasons to adopt the concept of Design – the most glaring reason being the tendency to fight the wrong problem. Typically, we end up fighting the last war or, worse yet, we end up fighting the plan. Human nature has a tendency to look for patterns that are familiar, and then to stay with that pattern even when reality doesn't match.

Design is intended to go beyond the standard approach – particularly in complex and ill-structured problems. For simple problems, design as a deliberate approach isn't necessary; for those simple problems, the solution is already apparent. For complex problems, design becomes extremely important; the more complex a situation, the more important design becomes.

In complex situations the elements of design help to establish coherence to responding to the situation: understanding the historical and cultural background of a situation; understanding the current context; envisioning the range of alternative futures and determining the desired end state; developing an operational approach / theory of action to bridge the gap between the current state of affairs and the future state of affairs; create a learning environment through collaboration and discourse; and continually assessing and reframing as the situation evolves.

Design goes beyond analyzing the "what" and "so what" of a problem – Design enables commanders and organizations to synthesize and evaluate data, going to the "which means" and "therefore" in operations and planning. In order to do this, Design incorporates not only looking at strengths, weaknesses, opportunities, and challenges... but also at interaction and system evolution and transformation.

Even though Design emphasizes the role of the commander, Design is a <u>team sport</u>. Design helps to "harvest the corporate intellect" of the commander, staff, superiors, and subordinates.

Commanders exercise collaborative leadership much as a football coach or the quarterback exercises leadership on the football team – everyone has a role to play with unique capabilities and contributions to make.

Of course, these concepts are not new; they have existed throughout history and are sprinkled throughout doctrine. Design complements existing processes, such as MDMP and JOPP. Design complements the operations process, including battle command and mission command. Design isn't conceptually limited to any particular echelon – it is equally useful at the tactical, operational, and strategic levels. Design can precede planning (before receipt of a formal mission), occur during planning, or take place while executing on-going operations.

Not using Design does entail a certain amount of risk. The *Issue Paper: Army Design Doctrine* (29 March 2009) identifies five areas of risk when leaders lack an explicit design methodology:

- Receiving guidance uncritically.

- Solving the wrong problem better.

- Misunderstanding the operational environment.

- Slower adaptation to changing circumstances.

- Failing to achieve designated goals.

RECEIVING GUIDANCE UNCRITICALLY: Higher political or military authorities frequently don't have all the answers; this is especially true in complex, ill-structured problems. Well-intentioned guidance from higher may frame a problem wrongly, and commanders at all levels must understand that greater understanding is normally achieved by those closer to the problem – lower to higher. Design emphasizes gaining and continually updating situation awareness, along with frequent collaboration and discourse to gain a shared understanding of a problem. Commanders can't arbitrarily disregard guidance from above, but they have an obligation to assess that guidance and to engage higher authorities for clarification and recommendations.

SOLVING THE WRONG PROBLEM BETTER: Throughout design, commanders need to continually ask if they are solving the right problem. The question, "What's the real story?" is a great question to ask throughout design, because it emphasizes getting to the root of problem rather than a symptom of a problem. The "real story" emphasizes understanding what is really going on, including interaction within the environment, the impact of history and culture, and competing interests. The same question also ponders whether the solution, or operational approach / theory of action, is really achieving the desired end state... and the question asks whether the desired end state is really the right answer. Constant assessment, reframing, and collaboration are techniques to get to the answer to the "real story." Without a deliberate design methodology, you may well have a great plan flawlessly executed – achieving the wrong ends.

MISUNDERSTANDING THE OPERATIONAL ENVIRONMENT: FM 3-0 states that conflict is fought "among the people." The human aspect of the operational environment must always be considered; the dynamic nature of human complexity is the key consideration in understanding the environment. Again, collaboration and discourse are key components to gain insight into the human dimension of the environment, drawing upon multiple perspectives, varied sources of knowledge, and subject matter experts. The operational environment must be analyzed considering not only the individual parts, but also as a coherent whole that has "emergent properties," enabling the environment to self-organize, adapt, and evolve.

SLOWER ADAPTATION TO CHANGING CIRCUMSTANCES: Just as the operational environment adapts and evolves, organizations adapt and evolve as circumstances change. An organization without a design methodology – focused on understanding the environment as it adapts and evolves – risks being slow to change accordingly. Continual learning, collaboration, and openness to reframing are essential to an organization's ability to adapt and evolve accordingly.

FAILING TO ACHIEVE DESIGNATED GOALS: Design provides an explicit link between strategy and tactics in order to integrate and coordinate operations. Without this linkage, tactical success may not translate into progress towards strategic goals. Reframing provides an opportunity to review the linkage between tactical actions and strategic goals, informed by collaboration among the echelons of war for a shared understanding of the operational approach and the desired end state.

> *"...the whole key lies very specifically in seeing it in the mind's eye – which we call visualization. The picture has to be there, clearly and decisively. If you have enough craft. If you have done your homework, you can then make the photograph you desire."*
>
> Ansel Adams

About the Author

Dr. Jack D. Kem retired as a colonel from the US Army in 1998, having served as a Field Artillery and Military Intelligence officer. He is currently the Commandant's Distinguished Chair of Military Innovation and Supervisory Professor, Department of Joint, Interagency, and Multinational Operations (DJIMO), U.S. Army Command and General Staff College, Fort Leavenworth, Kansas. He holds a B.A. from Western Kentucky University, an M.P.A. from Auburn University at Montgomery, and a Ph.D. from North Carolina State University. His current research interests include innovation, ethics, spirituality, military transformation, and campaign planning.

www.ingramcontent.com/pod-product-compliance
Lightning Source LLC
Chambersburg PA
CBHW070606290526
45790CB00002B/796